F₂

VANISHING
TRICK

by Brian Patten

POETRY
Little Johnny's Confession
Notes to The Hurrying Man
The Irrelevant Song

CHILDREN'S BOOKS
The Elephant and The Flower
Jumping Mouse
Mr. Moon's Last Case
Emma's Doll

Brian Patten

VANISHING
TRICK

London   George Allen & Unwin Ltd
Ruskin House   Museum Street

First published in 1976
by George Allen and Unwin (Publishers) Ltd.

ISBN 0 04 821037 4 hardback
     0 04 821038 2 paperback

ACKNOWLEDGEMENTS

Some of these poems first appeared in a limited
edition published by Bertram Rota Ltd. *You Missed
The Sunflowers At Their Height* was first published by
Turret Books, and *Sometimes It Happens* by Steam
Press as a broadsheet illustrated by Ralph Steadman.
The poem *Remembering* is based on several lines from
a poem by Victor Ouzin, translated from the Russian
by Kate Flemming.

Printed in Great Britain
in 12pt Goudy Type
by Butler & Tanner Ltd.
Frome and London

CONTENTS

7

A LOVE POEM

—— whose body has opened
Night after night
Harbouring loneliness,
Cancelling the doubts
Of which I am made,
Night after night
Taste me upon you.

Night and then again night,
And in your movements
The bed's shape is forgotten.
Sinking through it I follow,
Adrift on the taste of you.

I cannot speak clearly about you.
Night and then again night,
And after a night beside you
Night without you is barren.

I have never discovered
What alchemy makes
Your flesh different from the rest,
Nor why all that's commonplace
Comes to seem unique,

And though down my spine one answer leaks
It does not bother to explain itself.

9

The nerves tense up and then:
You have gone to sleep.
Something not anchored in love drifts out of reach.
You have gone to sleep, or feign sleep,
It does not matter which.
Into the voice leaks bitterness.
The throat dries up, the tongue
Swells with complaints.
Once sleep was simply sleep.
The future stretched no further than
The pillow upon which your head was resting,
There were no awkard questions in the world,
No doubts caused love to fade
To a numbed kiss or howl,
Or caused trust to vanish.
You have gone to sleep.
A moment ago I found
Your mouth on mine was counterfeit.
Your sleep is full of exhaustions,
I cannot calm you,
There is no potion to wake you.
Do what I will, say what I will,
It is a sleep from which I am exiled.
You have gone to sleep,
A planet drifts out of reach.
If I spoke all night it would be no use,
You would not wake,
And silence, like words, you would no doubt
Mistake for ignorance.
So sleep. Across our window's small patch of Heaven
The stars like sheep are herded,

And like a satellite objective time
Circles calendars and mocks
The wounds we think are huge.
Sleep, don't be so tense.
There is no longer a need of barriers,
No need of dumb defence.
You are understood.
This night is the last on which there will be
Any kind of pretence.
Tomorrow something else might wake
What's gone to sleep.

VANISHING TRICK

Your back is long and perfect, it is clear.
It moves away from me, it moves away,
    I watch it going.
In the morning I watch you gather up
longings mistakenly scattered.

I watch you gather up your face, your body,
watch till another creature walks about,
dressed and impatient.

You contained all there need be of love,
all there need be of jubilance and laughter you
    contained it.
And now you are its opposite,
you talk of going as if going were the smallest matter.

There do not have to be reasons for such changes,
there do not have to be.
In the morning bodies evaporate and nothing
can quite hold them together.

Suddenly everything changes.
Less than a second passes and nothing's the same.
Something that clung a moment ago lets go as if
all its clinging meant nothing.

Now in the bathroom the razors wait like a line
    of little friends,
they glow as much as roses,
they glow, glow with pain, with their own electricity,
they glow with darkness.

When you have gone they will turn their heads
    in my direction.
Inquisitive and eager they will welcome me,
but I will not listen.
I will try your vanishing trick and manage,
I will manage to feel nothing.

FORGETMEKNOT

She loves him, she loves him not, she is confused:
She picks a fist of soaking grass and fingers it:
She loves him not.
The message passing from her head to heart
Has in her stomach stopped,
She cannot quite believe the information is correct:
She loves him not.
She knows her needs and yet
There is no special place where they can rest.
To be loved alone is not enough,
She feels something has been lost.
She picks a fist of soaking grass.
Her world is blank, she thinks perhaps it's meaningless.

DRESSED

Dressed you are a different creature.
Dressed you are polite, are discreet and full of
    friendships,
Dressed you are almost serious.
You talk of the world and of all its disasters
As if they really moved you.
Dressed you hold on to illusions.

The wardrobes are full of your disguises.
The dress to be unbuttoned only in darkness,
The dress that seems always about to fall from you,
The touch-me-not dress, the how-expensive-dress,
The dress slung on without caring.
Dressed you are a different creature.

You are indignant of the eyes upon you,
The eyes that crawl over you,
That feed on the bits you've allowed
To be naked.
Dressed you are imprisioned in labels,
You are cocooned in fashions,
Dressed you are a different creature.

As easily as in the bedrooms
In the fields littered with rubble
The dresses fall from you,
In the spare room the party never reaches
The dresses fall from you.
Aided or unaided, clumsily or easily
The dresses fall from you and then
From you falls all the cheap blossom.
Undressed you are a different creature.

A BLADE OF GRASS

You ask for a poem.
I offer you a blade of grass.
You say it is not good enough.
You ask for a poem.

I say this blade of grass will do.
It has dressed itself in frost,
It is more immediate
Than any image of my making.

You say it is not a poem,
It is a blade of grass and grass
Is not quite good enough.
I offer you a blade of grass.

You are indignant.
You say it is too easy to offer grass.
It is absurd.
Anyone can offer a blade of grass.

You ask for a poem.
And so I write you a tragedy about
How a blade of grass
Becomes more and more difficult to offer,

And about how as you grow older
A blade of grass
Becomes more difficult to accept.

EMBROIDERED BUTTERFLIES

One afternoon you meet a young girl. She smiles at you,
It's summer and on the lakes the boats seem to burn.
She wears a dress through which you can see,
    Half-hidden by embroidered butterflies,
Her breasts, small and perfect.

She is attentive; she is going nowhere and shows
    How much she likes you.
Your routines fade again.
    The hedges smell good and glitter.

She is easy to get on with. Not for a long time
    has someone opened with such obvious pleasure.
You are glad it is summer, and can lounge in parks
    Or fall into rooms where she questions nothing.
For a moment she terrifies you with her freedom,
She's all over you laughing,
The dress she looked so good in earlier falls,
    Unashamedly, like petals.

Then in the evening the butterflies are worn again.
    You joke about them,
And when she laughs everything is changed —
    She is young and then is not so young.
You understand her freedom, how (like the butterflies)
It belongs to certain seasons, certain weathers.
    You are obsessed.
You ask her to stay, but it's evening and she says
    'It's not possible.' For one day only on your life
    Was this butterfly embroidered.

BELIEVING IN THE WALL

Blundering again, I found myself in a strange
   neighbourhood.
I walked into a cul-de-sac at the end of which
A familiar wall was waiting.
Behind me was a mess, a maze of spiritual failures,
Of blunderings nothing could alter.

To put right again all that had gone wrong
Was a dream I did not care for.
I sat on a stone beside the wall.
Memories spawned, their secrets stung me.

To wile away the time till some improbable event
   occurred
I took out my history and examined it.
On moss beside the stone I laid out my ambitions;
The awkward affairs, the imperfect insights.
To see them was a potion of kinds,
A way of understanding.

Beside the wall I made up fantasies.
I was sure all other streets led to neighbourhoods
   from which
All longings were banished,
Where at night in the bright halls
People danced like may-flies,
Where everything that ever ached had been replaced
By sensation too brief for pain.

Believing the wall real I sat beside it scheming.
Unintelligent dreamer, buffoon, I finally dreamed
A route through its bricks and found
A familiar wall was waiting.

YOU GO INTO TOWN

When she has gone you go into town.
You have learnt the places where the lonely go,
You know their habits, their acts of indifference
    practised so efficiently.
You have learnt how those who are hardly children
Can be most open, how the most obviously sensual
Tire you with questions; you have learnt
How inside them all
Terror is waiting.

At certain times the galleries close; in certain areas
    the supermarkets fill with strangers.
At certain times the bars swell with gossip,
    then people tire and look around.
Like one from another place and time
You've stepped through this ritual knowing
How on each face the promises are hollow,
How scarce any spontaneous greetings.

When she has gone you go into town.
But in no other face can you trace her,
In other bodies can be found
    Only an echo of her.
   You know the places where the lonely go,
You know their habits, their acts of indifference
    practised so efficiently.

READING BETWEEN THE GRAFFITI

On a toilet wall the graffiti's bleak—
'FUCK A STRANGER TONIGHT'
Reads a message not there last week.
Other slogans, names and boasts
Seem jaded compared with this
Advice scrawled by Anonymous.
But the graffiti evokes an image of the crowd,
The lost, androgynous animal
That does not die but daily swells,
That longs for kindness then reveals
A different nature on toilet walls.
Yet let's give its authors credit enough
To understand how the night
Breeds in its drunken scribblers
Things wrongly written that are right.

At night someone drifts through these walls
At night someone stands beside me saying
          Get up,
Get up from sleep, from the warm lull,
          Get up,
There is somewhere else to go.
Leave the womb behind you,
The womb in mint condition,
Leave it.
Leave it to its own fate,
Its prune fate.
          Get up.
The pillows smell of strangers;
All night the sheets howl.
          Get up
From the dead bed,
From the bed your mouth slaughtered.
You stink of nightmares,
          Get up,
There is somewhere else to go,
Somewhere not sucked dry,
Somewhere that does not terrify.
          Get up,
The heart has gone fat and blind.
While you slept
Paradise shrank to a single leaf.
Nightly and inevitably
I reach into the darkness to touch him,
And touching only my own flesh
   I creep in terror from the bed's grave.

Get up,
No doubt through these walls at night
Your own stranger drifts,
Invisible to me, mouthing the same message;
Let's get up,
We have listened so often saying nothing
That we have become the phantoms.

NIGHT PIECE

All day I have spent building this web,
This necessary extension strung between
Objects unfamiliar and uncertain.
Over those things to which it is anchored
I have no power. My trust must be explicit.
So far I have caught rain, sunlight,
Particles of leaf, and things so small
They cannot satisfy.
At night in a crack between concrete
I dream of catching something so immense
It would shake the web's centre;
Awkward and meat-ridden, its wings
Would snap and dullen my creation.
Of such an event I am terrified,
For such an event I am longing.

ON TIME FOR ONCE

I was sitting thinking of our future
    and of how friendship had overcome
so many nights bloated with pain;

    I was sitting in a room that looked on to a garden
and a stillness filled me,
    bitterness drifted from me.

I was as near paradise as I am likely to get again.

    I was sitting thinking of the chaos
we had caused in one another
    and was amazed we had survived it.

I was thinking of our future
    and of what we would do together,
and where we would go and how,

    when night came
burying me bit by bit,
    and you entered the room

trembling and solemn-faced,
    on time for once.

LEAVETAKING

She grew careless with her mouth.
Her lips came home in the evening numbed.
Excuses festered among her words.
She said one thing, her body said another.
Her body, exhausted, spoke the truth.
She grew careless, or became without care,
Or panicked between both.

Too logical to suffer, imagining
Love short-lived and 'forever'
A lie fostered on the mass to light
Blank days with hope,
What she meant to me was soon diminished.
I too had grown careless with my mouth.
Habit wrecked us both, and wrecked
We left the fragments untouched, and left.

THE ASSASSINATION OF THE MORNING

The morning has a hole in its side,
It rolls through the grass like a wounded bear,
Over and over it goes, clutching its wound,
Its wound fat with sorrow.

I feel nothing for the morning.
I kneel in the early grass and stare out blankly;
I stare at the blank leaves,
The leaves fat with sorrow.

Morning, the birds have come to patch you up.
They will bandage you with grass.
Morning, you are so tired.
Your eyes look terrible.

I remember how once
You were so eager to begin life,
Dressed in glittering frost you strolled
Nonchalantly down the avenues.

O Morning, it was bound to happen;

You grasp at the wet branches, the spikey thickets.
Over and over you roll, the years pouring out of you.
I wipe a razor clean of flowers, ignore the birds,
and their insistent shouting of 'Assassin'.

AND NOTHING IS EVER AS PERFECT
AS YOU WANT IT TO BE

You lose your love for her and then
It is her who is lost,
And then it is both who are lost,
And nothing is ever as perfect as you want it to be.

In a very ordinary world
A most extraordinary pain mingles with the small
    routines,
The loss seems huge and yet
Nothing can be pinned down or fully explained.

You are afraid.
If you found the perfect love
It would scald your hands,
Rip the skin from your nerves,
Cause havoc with a computed heart.

You lose your love for her and then it is her who is lost.
You tried not to hurt and yet
Everything you touched became a wound.
You tried to mend what cannot be mended,
You tried, neither foolish nor clumsy,
To rescue what cannot be rescued.

You failed,
And now she is elsewhere
And her night and your night
Are both utterly drained.

How easy it would be
If love could be brought home like a lost kitten
Or gathered in like strawberries,
How lovely it would be;
But nothing is ever as perfect as you want it to be.

A SUITCASE FULL OF DUST

I packed a suitcase.
I put dust in it.
And then more dust.
I packed bits and pieces
Of what was still living.

I packed a suitcase.
A heart howled inside it.
A face stared up from it,
Its tongue wagging in the dust.

With each passing second
The complaints it made
Seemed more obsolete.
I packed a suitcase full of dust.

I went outside.
I was afraid people would stop me and ask
Why I was travelling about with dust.

There seemed nowhere to go
But to another place of dust.
I do not want dust.
My blood is slow and full of dust.
And your kiss is dust.

I do not want dust.
Your breath has changed
Pollen into dust.
I do not want dust.

Swearing fidelity to all
That is clean and free of dust
I pack a suitcase full of dust.

NO TAXIS AVAILABLE

It is absurd not knowing where to go.

You wear the streets like an overcoat.
Certain houses are friends, certain houses
Can no longer be visited.
Old love-affairs lurk in doorways, behind windows
Women grow older. Neglection blossoms.

You have turned down numerous invitations,
Left the telephones unanswered, said 'No'
To the few that needed you.
Stranded on an island of your own invention
You have thrown out messages, longings.

How useless it is knowing that where you want to go
Is nowhere concrete.
The trains will not take you there,
The red buses glide past without stopping,

No taxis are available.

'IF YOU HAD TO HAZARD A GUESS, WHO WOULD YOU SAY YOUR POETRY IS FOR?'

For people who have nowhere to go in the afternoons,
    for people who the evening banishes to small rooms,
for good people, people huge as the world.
    For people who give themselves away forgetting
what it is they are giving,
    and who are never reminded.
For people who cannot help being kind
    to the hand bunched in pain against them.
For inarticulate people,
    people who invent their own ugliness,
who invent pain, terrified of blankness;
    and for people who stand forever at the same
        junctions
waiting for the chances that have passed.
    And for people who lie in ambush for themselves,
    who invent toughness as a kind of disguise,
who, lost in their narrow and self-
    defeating worlds,
carry remorse inside them like a plague;
and for the self-seeking self lost among them
    I hazard a poem.

WINTER NOTE

It's evening and the streets are cold again.
The cars go past in such a hurry you'd think
The world full of emergencies.
The young men and women no longer parading
Hurry from the supermarkets,
Feigning a lack of caring, their tins
Glow with loneliness.
Leaves gone, scents gossip of previous winters.

And what did we do then?
Were the florists' windows stuffed with bright icy
  flowers?
Were the sirens as persistent, the parks as barren?
Whose hand was held, whose face
Did we swear never to forget?

As always the rooms are damp, the furniture ancient.
Yet among this drabness is a light, self-created.
The wine stains on the carpet emerge as roses,
The fridge becomes a grotto.
We fill our heads with dreams still.
In this season we are all that blossoms.

SIMPLE LYRIC

When I think of her sparkling face
And of her body that rocked this way and that,
When I think of her laughter,
Her jubilance that filled me,
It's a wonder I'm not gone mad.

She is away and I cannot do what I want.
Other faces pale when I get close.
She is away and I cannot breathe her in.

The space her leaving has created
I have attempted to fill
With bodies that numbed upon touching,
Among them I expected her opposite,
And found only forgeries.

Her wholeness I know to be a fiction of my making,
Still I cannot dismiss the longing for her;
It is a craving for sensation new flesh
Cannot wholly calm or cancel,
It is perhaps for more than her.

At night above the parks the stars are swarming.
The streets are thick with nostalgia;
I move through senseless routine and insensitive
    chatter
As if her going did not matter.
She is away and I cannot breath her in,
I am ill simply through wanting her.

SOMETIMES IT HAPPENS

And sometimes it happens that you are friends and
  then
You are not friends,
And friendship has passed.
And whole days are lost and among them
A fountain empties itself.

And sometimes it happens that you are loved and
  then
You are not loved,
And love is past.
And whole days are lost and among them
A fountain empties itself into the grass.

And sometimes you want to speak to her and then
You do not want to speak,
Then the opportunity has passed.
Your dreams flare up, they suddenly vanish.

And also it happens that there is nowhere to go and
  then
There is somewhere to go,
Then you have bypassed.
And the years flare up and are gone,
Quicker than a minute.

So you have nothing.
You wonder if these things matter and then
They cease to matter,
And caring is past.
And a fountain empties itself into the grass.

THE MISTAKE

Because we passed grief to and fro
toying with it,
I have shut the door of this room,

I have shut out everyone else's pain
until I can cope with my own;
tonight I'm confused enough.

For too long I have been
one of this city's strays,
yelping for attention,

part of that mass disfigured
through self-inflicted pain,
its flesh washed by exhaustion.

Because there is no pill or science
to dismiss the darkness
that is given like a gift

I have shut the door of this room;
but that too is a mistake of kinds,
for the room is in darkness,

and sinking deeper into it
the mistake becomes obvious.

REMEMBERING

Not all that you want and ought not to want
Is forbidden to you,
Not all that you want and are allowed to want
Is acceptable.
Then it gets late on
And things change their value.

You are tired.
You feel the ground with your hands.
A single blade of grass appears before your eyes.
It flashes on and off,
a remnant of paradise.

And then perhaps you will remember
What you have forgotten to remember,
What should have been so easy remembering.

You will recall the hut in the morning,
And how the hoof-prints were flooded with frost,
And how a weed and a pebble were caught once
On a cow's lip,

And perhaps how on a tremendous horse
A small boy once galloped off,
And how it was possible to do
All that now seems impossible,
All you ever wanted.

SLEEPY

Sleepy, you had nothing to tell me.
Yet in such moments was no song
Nor sound nor laugh nor anything so pure
As the silence with which you presented me.
Spilt over into oblivion and then spilt back again,
You came back speechless.
O planet face! I still smell the forest in your neck!
Still taste the stream in your mouth!
And your kiss that dropped on to my skin like rain
Still shivers there!

THE STOLEN ORANGE

When I went out I stole an orange
I kept it in my pocket
It felt like a warm planet

Everywhere I went smelt of oranges
Whenever I got into an awkward situation
I'd take the orange out and smell it

And immediately on even dead branches I saw
The lovely and fierce orange blossom
That smells so much of joy

When I went out I stole an orange
It was a safeguard against imagining
there was nothing bright or special in the world

TOWARDS EVENING AND TIRED OF
THE PLACE

Time to uproot again, there's much to be cancelled;
Your dreams, like useless trinkets, have come to
    nothing.
Across the harbour the lights have dullened,
In the town rain's scattered petals.
You are vague now about what things matter.
The years have ceased to preen themselves in front
    of mirrors,
The cafes do not always glitter, the women sit
Big-eyed and drained of laughter.
From their breasts you have detached your dreams,
They would have aged there.

You have shrugged off the moments in your life
When things have begun to matter,
Preferring to remain weightless,
Adrift in places where nothing has yet happened.
Believing there are better things than the best,
Brighter things than the brightest,
You have alighted like a butterfly
    on insubstantial flowers,
Have wasted your life in conversations with yourself,
Moved so long within your own shadow
That no weight can be felt, no commitments made.
Over all the world the rain falls like an answer.

LETHARGY

You have dreamt so often of what you would do
If your life were irrevocably changed
    That when you are forced finally from the route
        best understood
And on to another, less obvious way,
    You think at first fantasy will sustain you.
Sink then dreamer into what might have been!
    For though on the brilliant branch
The brilliant fruit still clings
    It is no longer reached with ease,
And its dazzle's frightening.

HER ADVICE

She said, 'Come from the window,
Dreamer, do not drift too far from me;
In other rooms the party's growing old.
Leave off star-gazing for a time,
Leave Heaven to dance alone.
Come from the window;
Dreamer, unlike myself,
Heaven left alone will not grow bored.
The wonder you seek there
You yourself when younger formed'.
And she was right.
Though our longings do not end with what she says,
She was right. Without her help
Night would have been simply night,
The stars of little consequence, and not very bright.

AFTER FROST

It's hard to tell what bird it is
Singing in the misty wood,
Or the reason for its song
So late after evening's come.

When all else has dropped its name
Down into the scented dark
Its song grown cool and clear says
Nothing much to anyone,

But catches hold a whisper in my brain
That only now is understood.
It says, rest your life against this song,
It's rest enough for anyone.

'Suckablood, Suckablood, where have you been?'
'I've been in the brain of a Dreaming Machine.'

'Suckablood, Suckablood, what did you there?'
'I taught it of sorrow and loss, pain and despair.'

'Suckablood, Suckablood, were the lessons much
fun?'
'I spoke sombrely of all that is soon come and
soon gone.'

'Suckablood, Suckablood, does it know what
you've done!?'
'I think it has some inkling of what has begun.'

'If it wants no more lessons, then what's to be done?'
'Don't worry, to me I am sure it will come.'

'Suckablood, Suckablood, what if it's late?'
'Then in the grave my lessons will keep.'

TURNING THE PAGES

Late at night I sat turning the pages,
half-looking for the lines I had once read
astonished at their simplicity.
Late at night I sat turning the pages,
my tongue uprooting miniature lights, infatuated
with what it hoped to become.
I sat turning the pages ignoring
the voices that asked,
    'What answers can be found by simply turning
    the pages,
late at night turning the pages looking
for the lines you once read?'
While the future amassed its griefs
and things left undone squabbled and multiplied
I sat turning the pages,
    And slowly I learned
how to abandon the future
and leave it less crowded,
    and I understood
how there is nothing complicated in the world
that is not of my own making,
    and how for years I had lived
under the scrutiny of the blind,
believing they could see me best.
I lacked confidence not in what I was
but in what others considered me.
Now I am glad I lacked such confidence,
and sat late at night turning the pages
half-looking for the lines I had once read,
astonished at their simplicity.

A DROP OF UNCLOUDED BLOOD

All day I will think of these cities floating fragile
across the earth's crust
and of how they are in need
of a drop of magic blood
a drop of unclouded blood

All day I will think of snow and the small
violets like a giant's blood
splashed at random on the earth
All day I will stroll about hoping
for a drop of unclouded blood
to fall into my veins

I need my body to move loose through the world
Need my fingers to touch the skin
of children adrift in their temporary world
Beneath their dreaming is a drop of blood
refusing the sun's heat
a drop of blood more pure than any other blood

I need to walk through the pale light
that occupies the world
and believe it when a drop of blood says
Listen,
paradise is never far away
and simpler than you think it

I need to sever all connection with the habits
that make the heart
love only certain things
I need a drop of magic blood for that
a drop of unclouded blood

NEWS FROM THE GLADLAND

Falling into the green and outstretched palm of the
    world
the messenger is visible and is heard to sing:

'Today I bring you good news, the same good news as ever:
Down by the wide lakes the giant suns have risen,
Lighting the sails of boats going outwards forever.

Today I bring you good news, the same good news as ever:
Autumn's sailors, disappearing over the rim of the world,
Are not lost nor drowned nor crying.
Their mouths are stuffed with apples.
Their bodies are cool as the morning's grasses.
Their lungs are opened up like flowers.

And today I bring you strange news, the same strange
    news as ever:
This country will never be lost,
Every morning it is born afresh,
Every morning it is born forever,
Yet the children who cross it laughing
(O strangest of mammals!)
Will not return if their sight is ruined.

And today I bring you good advice, simple advice the
    same as ever:
You must celebrate the morning in your blood,
For nothing dies there, nothing ends,
Over and over again you must invent yourselves,
True magicians, riding the senses of dust,
Know that with this gift you're blest.'

YOU MISSED THE SUNFLOWERS AT
THEIR HEIGHT

You missed the sunflowers at their height,
Came back when they were bent and worn
And the gnats, half-froze, fell one by one
Into the last of the sprawling marigolds.

And as if linked to some spider thread
Made visible only because of rain,
You sat and watched the day come light
And hope leapt back into your brain,

And suddenly this surprising earth
No longer clouded, was known again,
And all you had thought lost you found
Was simply for a time mislaid.

SONG ABOUT HOME

I have gone out, making a pathway through the
    morning,
Gone out, ankle-deep in silence,
Never to come back this way.
My brain wears a lining of frost, it sparkles,
My way is clear enough.

Call memory forest, and all the things that ever
    stunned,
The roots of that forest,
Fed by voices so previous
The rain cannot shake them out, nor seasons cancel.
The stars are alive in me,
They go about like drunken satellites.

I'm obsessed, and the obsessions gladden.
I have gone to where the ant goes,
To where the bird whistles.
I follow the vast pathway a snail makes,
Drift unaware through the white dandelions.

Through negligence most friendships have faded,
But what does it matter?
There was never one place I belonged in.
I sing of how home is the place not yet visited,
Built out of longings, mapped out by accidents.

I TRIED TO FIND MY VOICE

I tried to find my voice, a voice lost
In a night thickened by paranoia,
In a night crowded out by doubts
It could not articulate.
I had let go of it through negligence,
As at a carnival one lets go a child's hand.

I rummaged through a jumble sale of bodies,
Listened to advice devoid of meaning;
My voice was like a moth, its few colours
Worn to exhaustion.
It was drunk and lost, it was battered
And flung everywhere.

I tried to find it in the beds
Of solemn girls disguised as women,
I tried to find it among the men I envied.
I searched for it among its own inventions.

I had arranged my life around that voice.
Absurdly relied on it to explain
Who and what I was,
As if either mattered.
In strange towns I used it to advantage.
Whatever it could fish out from the night
I accepted.

No matter; it was the one voice I let delude me.
Maybe it was getting the better of me,
Maybe it was envious and screamed at times,
Certainly it said things of which I'd grown ashamed,

But I forgave it its blindness and tantrums
Hoping it would change.

And now it is beyond change.
My mouth cannot find it.
I have lost it; and no longer wish it back.
In winter I will make a voice out of snow,
In spring I will make a voice out of flowers,
In summer and autumn I will make a voice
With what is at hand.

The complaints it carried like credentials are misplaced
And its mouthful of reasons are blown away,
And its mouthful of tragedies
Have become light as dandelion seeds.

ONE ANOTHER'S LIGHT

It's hard to guess what brought me here,
Away from where I've hardly ever been and now
Am never likely to go again.

Faces are lost, and places passed
At which I could have stopped
And stopping, been glad enough.

Some faces left a mark;
And I on them might have wrought
Some kind of charm or spell
To make their futures work,

But it's hard to guess
How one thing on another
Works an influence.
We pass—
And lit briefly by one another's light
Think the way we go is right.